# 19TH CENTURY AMERICAN HISTORY FOR KIDS

# 19th CENTURY AMERICAN HISTORY

## FOR *Kids*

### the MAJOR EVENTS that SHAPED the PAST and PRESENT

KELLY MILNER HALLS

callisto
publishing
an imprint of Sourcebooks

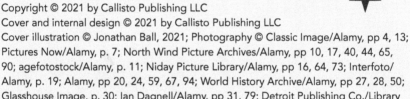

THIS BOOK IS DEDICATED TO MY
PARENTS, WHO HELPED BUILD
THE COUNTRY'S PAST, AND TO
MY CHILDREN, WHO HAVE BEEN
ENTRUSTED WITH ITS FUTURE.

# CONTENTS

# INTRODUCTION

**W**hen you were a baby, your caretakers tried to teach you the meaning of the word "hot." You didn't *really* understand until you burned your fingers on a steaming bowl of soup or a birthday candle.

Your history as a little person taught you a lesson you will probably remember the rest of your life: "Hot" can hurt.

The study of American history is a lot like that first burned finger. If we understand what happened in the past, we can use the lessons to build a better future. And the 19th century–which started in 1801 and ended in 1900–was an era full of powerful lessons.

As the 18th century (the 1700s) ended, the United States of America was still a very young nation, learning how to live by laws written by the people instead of commands set down by a king across the sea.

In the first year of the 19th century, Thomas Jefferson was elected the third American president. Two years later, Ohio became the 17th American state.

Freedom was in the air, but so was injustice. As explorers headed west to claim new territory for the country, Indigenous Peoples, who at the time were called "Indians," were pushed from their homelands. Enslaved African people suffered under white landowners who wrongly believed human beings could be property.

Change was possible—and essential. During the 19th century, many important changes to make the United States a more fair and just nation were introduced, but real and lasting progress takes time. So history reminds us that patience and determination will help us avoid mistakes we might regret.

Studying history can help us keep the dream of improvement alive. If we learn the lessons of the past, we can grow stronger, wiser, and kinder—as individuals and as a nation.

This book will not describe every important event of the 19th century, but it will introduce you to some of the key moments and players. If we understand how previous generations lived, we'll be able to build on their progress.

# AMERICA AT THE TURN OF THE CENTURY

As citizens of a new nation, Americans began to establish their own new traditions. The **Revolutionary War**, which ended in 1783, had secured their independence from England. Since King George III and his government no longer controlled how the colonists would live, they could build a future of their own.

The United States Constitution and the Bill of Rights would help guide the creation and enforcement of new laws. And those new laws would impact every other aspect of American existence, from religion and architecture to fashion, literature, music, and art.

The United States of America was a blank canvas. Almost anything seemed possible ... or at least it did for wealthy white men.

Women and people of color didn't enjoy the same freedoms that educated white men did after the revolution. But hope had taken root. If freedom was possible for one class of new America, they thought, it might one day be possible for all Americans.

Even today, no one knows how the rest of the American story will play out. But its beginnings were full of energy and expanding promise.

# CHAPTER ONE

# 1801
## TO
# 1820

**When Thomas Jefferson helped write the** Declaration of Independence in 1776, he called for the brutal practice of slavery to end, even while he himself benefited from it. But South Carolina and Georgia objected to Jefferson's plan to free enslaved people.

And so slavery continued, even after America claimed its independence and elected Jefferson its third president in 1800. Still forced to work without rights or wages, the enslaved Africans suffered at the hands of enslavers as the 19th century began. But they continued to dream.

Enslaved people had seen America's escape from the harsh rule of a king. Perhaps freedom was possible for them, too. After all, the United States of America was a big country and it was getting bigger every day.

The rush to claim the continent's western territories had begun. But that expansion had its own problems. If the western territories became American states, what would happen to the Indigenous Peoples who had called this land home for generations?

And America wasn't the only country staking a claim on the land. Britain, France, and Spain all wanted a piece of North and South America.

Revolution had defeated King George, but there were new struggles ahead. Lasting peace was decades away, and it would come at an enormous cost.

The slave trade in America

# Gabriel's Rebellion: 1800

Gabriel was born into slavery in 1776 on the Thomas Prosser plantation near Richmond, Virginia. A plantation is a large farm that uses slave labor to take care of crops and agriculture such as cotton, tobacco, and sugar, so they can be sold. Trained as a blacksmith, Gabriel was hired out to wealthy homes and businesses for extra income. Most of the money went to Prosser, but Gabriel was allowed to keep a small portion for himself.

Gabriel was given more freedom than most enslaved people: He was taught to read and was allowed to leave the plantation without supervision. He could talk with free men in Richmond, who shared bold ideas of freedom for enslaved Black people.

On the plantation, life was hard. Afraid he and his older brothers might starve, Gabriel tried to steal a pig from the neighboring plantation. He was caught red-handed by the white plantation foreman.

The two men fought, and in the heat of the moment, Gabriel bit off a chunk of the foreman's left ear. Stealing a pig was punishable with a beating, but attacking a white man meant death.

Prosser didn't want to lose the money Gabriel could earn, so he paid a fine and allowed the neighbor to whip Gabriel in public. After the lashing, Gabriel's hand was branded with a burning hot tool to mark him as a troublemaker.

After this punishment, Gabriel's desire for freedom grew stronger. With the help of his enslaved friends,

## MEET JAMES MONROE

Born into a wealthy Virginia family in 1758, James Monroe joined the Continental Army to fight for the colonies' freedom from England when he was seventeen. He became the fifth president of the United States in 1816. As a member of the American Colonization Society, James hoped enslaved Africans in America might one day be relocated to Liberia, on the African continent. But this idea has left a complicated legacy.

he planned a **rebellion**. On Saturday, August 30, 1800, twenty-four-year-old Gabriel and his secret army stormed Richmond and took Governor James Monroe hostage. They demanded that he free all Virginia slaves.

His plan might have worked, but Gabriel was betrayed by two frightened friends and confessed. Ten of Gabriel's allies were sentenced to death and hanged, including his two brothers. Sixteen more died soon after.

Gabriel was arrested a few days later, hiding on a ship on the James River. He was hanged on October 10, 1800, and his body was buried in a cemetery for enslaved people in Richmond.

During the 19th century, many enslaved people fought for freedom, and like Gabriel, their dreams of freedom were usually dashed. But their determination gave their fellow enslaved people hope.

## HOW MANY ENSLAVED PEOPLE?

From 1525 to 1808, roughly 12.5 million Africans were brought in dark, crowded ships into slavery. Only 10.7 million survived the punishing ocean passage. Of the survivors, about 388,000 were originally sold to North American owners. But a thriving international slave trade sent that number soaring as high as seven million before slavery was outlawed.

Discussing the purchase of New Orleans

# The Louisiana Purchase: 1803

In 1682, French explorer René-Robert Cavelier de La Salle claimed 828,000 square miles of North American land for King Louis XIV. In honor of the King, Cavelier named the territory Louisiana. It ran from the Gulf of Mexico, all the way up the west banks of the Mississippi River to the north, then west to the Rocky Mountains.

In 1763, King Louis XV gave Louisiana to his cousin, King Charles III of Spain. King Charles valued the city of New Orleans as a port for international trade, but he had little interest in the rest of the territory, and he allowed the Caddo, Biloxi, Chitimacha, and Choctaw

## MEET TOUSSAINT L'OUVERTURE

In 1743, François Toussaint L'Ouverture was born into slavery on the island of Saint-Domingue—now known as Haiti. A devoted Catholic, he saw slavery as a sin, and led a revolution to free the Black population from their French captors. The revolt was a success, but L'Ouverture died sick and alone in a French prison cell in 1803.

tribal nations to keep their traditional homelands.

Spain soon decided Louisiana was too expensive to maintain, so French **dictator** Napoléon Bonaparte took it back in 1800. Napoléon set his sights on Saint-Domingue, now known as Haiti. Enslaved Africans who once made French colonists rich producing sugar and coffee had rebelled and sent their French enslavers running. Napoléon planned to take it back.

With Louisiana back under French control, Napoléon could supply his troops on Haiti more easily. And Louisiana would also make it possible for the French to claim more North American land to colonize.

President Thomas Jefferson was concerned about French troops gathering in New Orleans. He feared Napoléon would block American trade in New

Orleans. And he feared French soldiers might launch new wars. So, Jefferson sent James Monroe to France to buy the city of New Orleans. He approved up to $9,375,000 to make the deal.

The war had been expensive and his troops were sick, so Napoléon was ready to make a deal. He hoped to fund a war that he was fighting against other European powers, and selling land in the Americas was a good way to do it. He demanded $15 million dollars—but he offered the entire Louisiana territory, not just the city of New Orleans, for that price.

After securing a loan from Great Britain in 1803, Jefferson made the Louisiana Purchase and nearly doubled the size of the United States. This land would go on to make up all or part of 15 states.

## AN INDIGENOUS SANCTUARY?

**Historian James E. Lewis Jr. says that Jefferson wanted to make the land from the Louisiana Purchase into "a preserve for Native Americans." But when asked to move from the western banks of the Mississippi River to the eastern banks to make it possible, the citizens of St. Louis refused. What might have been a chance for Americans to live peacefully among Indigenous People faded away.**

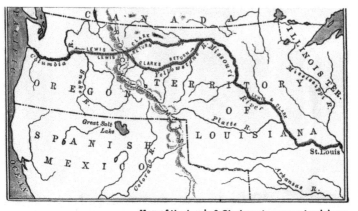

**Map of the Lewis & Clark route across Louisiana**

# Lewis & Clark Expedition: 1804

Even before Thomas Jefferson made the Louisiana Purchase, he hired Meriwether Lewis to explore the western wilderness for scientific purposes. But the task took on greater importance when the territory became a part of the United States.

Meriwether studied existing maps, medicine, **botany**, astronomy, and zoology to prepare for the adventure. He then hired his friend William Clark to help make the long journey.

Together, they gathered supplies, including a 55-foot barge, two smaller boats, weapons, medicine, compasses, telescopes, fishing equipment, soap, and salt. They also brought gifts to offer any Indigenous

Peoples they met along the way.

Next, they hired the Corp of Discovery—27 healthy, unmarried young men, an interpreter, and a boat crew to make the continental crossing.

On May 14, 1804, the expedition launched on the Missouri River. It covered 15 miles a day on the water, battling insects, bad weather, and dangerous river currents at every turn. A month in, expedition member Charles Floyd died of an intestinal illness, but he was the only member of the team lost.

Lewis and Clark connected with more than 50 different Indigenous tribes as they moved west, including the Shoshone, the Mandan, the Hidatsa, the Blackfeet, and the Lakota. Some were eager to

## MEET SACAJAWEA

Sacajawea, the daughter of a Shoshone **chief** in Idaho, was taken to North Dakota by the Hidatsa Nation as a twelve-year-old. Along with her native tongue, she learned the language of her captors. Being **bilingual** made her a valuable member of the Corp of Discovery when she joined Lewis and Clark's expedition. And a woman's presence convinced tribal leaders that the expedition was peaceful.

trade with the explorers. Some were suspicious of the strangers. But violence struck only once: When Blackfeet warriors tried to steal expedition horses in Montana, Clark was shot in the backside but survived. Two Blackfeet citizens died in the gun battle.

By November of 1805, the expedition had made it to the Pacific Ocean on what is now the coast of Oregon. When they returned to St. Louis on September 23, 1806, they were celebrated as heroes.

In the fall of 1806, Lewis and Clark briefed President Jefferson on their discoveries. Across 8,000 miles, they mapped an expansive new territory, offered friendly introductions to Indigenous Peoples, and documented dozens of new species of plants and animals.

The most ambitious scientific exploration in America's history was a success.

## MEDALS OF FRIENDSHIP

Lewis and Clark carried 89 silver medals to offer tribal leaders. Thirty-two "Jefferson Peace" medals had the president's face on one side and a handshake on the other. Fifty-seven "Washington Season" medals featured George Washington. The gifts were meant to convince the Indigenous Peoples that America would be a peaceful ally.

Enslaved people in the 19th century

# End of the Slave Trade: 1808

For most of the 18th century, slavery was a common practice in most of the 13 colonies. In fact, slavery—the practice of holding people captive and forcing them to do unpaid labor—has existed in many parts of the world throughout human history.

But the institution of slavery in America was unusually cruel and hard to escape. In other parts of the world, including Africa, enslaved people enjoyed basic **human rights**. They could marry, own land, and testify in legal disagreements. They were valued by their enslavers, even treated as family. Those things were not true for most Africans enslaved in America.

By 1807, more than four million people were being forced to work for white men throughout the American South. They lived in horrible conditions, without pay, decent nutrition, safe living quarters, or medical assistance—without any freedoms at all.

Once born, the children of enslaved people could be sold for any reason at all. Families were torn apart when husbands, wives, brothers, and sisters were bought and sold. The enslavers did not care about the feelings of the enslaved—only about the money and labor that they could get from slave trading.

To the slaveholders, enslaved people were not human beings. They were treated like livestock, like horses or cattle. They were stripped of their human rights and denied any sense of dignity.

The tides seemed to be turning in January of 1807, when the United States Congress passed an act to block the importation of kidnapped human beings from "any foreign kingdom, place, or country." But although the new legislation banned the import of new enslaved people from Africa, the trade of enslaved people already in America did not stop. To increase their numbers, enslavers forced their slaves to have babies of their own.

The new law of 1808 ended the practice of rounding up new foreign enslaved people, but turned a blind eye to the cruelty against people already enslaved in North America. This was a question that haunted people of good conscience until the entire institution of slavery was abolished after the Civil War.

## SLAVERY BY THE NUMBERS

By 1810, the original 13 American colonies had purchased and enslaved over one million people from Africa. Virginia enslaved the most people, with 392,518. Massachusetts and New Hampshire had the fewest, at zero.

Battle of Tippecanoe in November, 1811

# The Battle of Tippecanoe: 1811

As the US population expanded westward from the original British colonies, white settlers relocated to land that had long been occupied by Indigenous Peoples.

Some of the new settlers were content to share the land and the natural resources with the Indigenous Peoples, but many more pushed them out of their ancestral homelands. The Battle of Tippecanoe was an example of how that friction could explode into bloodshed.

William Henry Harrison was the governor of the Indiana Territory. The Shawnee tribe, led by Tecumseh and his brother Tenskwatawa, also lived on the land. The Shawnee were part of a group of tribes that opposed American and European settlement of the West.

In 1811, as tensions rose between the white settlers and the tribes, Harrison was sure he could

MEET TECUMSEH

As a boy, Tecumseh witnessed horrible attacks against his people, the Shawnee, at the hands of white American settlers. But he also saw the needless slaughter of white people. He was opposed to both, so he proposed a solution: The Native Nations would unite to demand a safe homeland. When the solution failed, Tecumseh fought against the United States and died for his people.

defeat Tecumseh and his brother as they tried to unite local tribes. He planned a surprise attack against their headquarters on the Tippecanoe Creek, but the brothers had a surprise of their own.

Before Harrison could strike, Tecumseh launched a pre-dawn raid on the American forces. The battle lasted just three hours. There were many deaths on both sides, but the Americans claimed victory. Tecumseh and his followers moved north to join British Canadians, while his brother Tenskwatawa continued working to unite the tribes of the Indiana Territory against the American and European settlers.

The friction of the Battle of Tippecanoe led directly to an **alliance** between Indigenous Peoples and Britain in the War of 1812 six months later, when the United States went to war, once again, against Great Britain. The **Treaty** of Ghent, which ended the war in 1814, called for an end to all wars with Indigenous Peoples, but the Americans largely ignored that directive. The United States continued warring against Indigenous Peoples for the rest of the 19th century.

## THE FIRST AMERICANS

**Some people believe Indigenous People have always lived on the North American continent. Others say Asian people walked across the prehistoric Bering Strait—an ice bridge from Russia to Alaska—then migrated south. A few believe Asian people traveled by boat along the "Kelp Highway" to migrate to the Americas. Without conclusive evidence, the truth remains a mystery.**

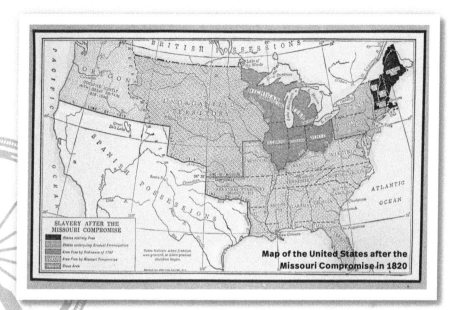

Map of the United States after the Missouri Compromise in 1820

# The Missouri Compromise: 1820

In December of 1819, the United States included 22 states. Eleven were free states—meaning slavery was illegal—and eleven allowed slavery. That even count created a balance in American government. Neither side could seriously impact the other when it came to the creation of new laws about slavery, and so an uneasy peace was maintained.

All that changed when Missouri, a slave-holding territory, wanted to become the 23rd state. If they were granted statehood, the balance would shift and the slave states would have more power than the free states. That was a problem.

James Tallmadge Jr. was born in 1778 in New York. He studied law at Brown University in Rhode Island and fought in the War of 1812. Once elected to the United States Congress, he became a vocal abolitionist, a person opposed to slavery. His Tallmadge Amendment might have ended slavery in the country without war. But the law was not passed.

A Congressman from New York named James Tallmadge Jr. was an **abolitionist**, meaning he wanted to end the practice of slavery. So he suggested a special **amendment**. He proposed that all new slave states could allow the ownership of people that were already enslaved until they passed away. But new people born after 1819 would be automatically free American citizens once they turned twenty-five years old.

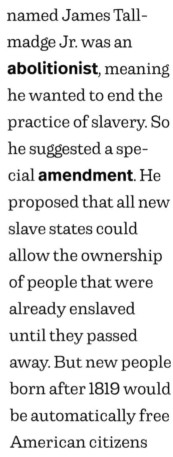

The Tallmadge Amendment would have ended slavery gradually in all new US slave states, as older enslaved persons died and younger ones came of age. The House of Representatives voted to pass the Tallmadge Amendment, but the Senate did not.

They were back at square one, so Henry Clay, a Senator from Kentucky, offered a different compromise.

He proposed that Missouri be admitted as a slave state, as they requested. But the large state of Massachusetts, a free state, could be divided in two to create the new free state of Maine. That would preserve the fragile balance.

Clay also suggested that any new states admitted north of the latitude 36°30' would need to be free states. And any new states below that boundary would be allowed to keep slaves.

Clay's solution became law and was known as the Missouri Compromise. It kept the peace, temporarily. But former President Thomas Jefferson knew it was just a matter of time before the anger between the two sides reached a boiling point and threatened the grand experiment of American democracy.

The Civil War would soon prove Jefferson right.

## KANSAS-NEBRASKA ACT OF 1854

**The angry debate over slavery would take an explosive turn in 1854 with the Kansas-Nebraska Act. Meant to end the Missouri Compromise, it sought to strengthen the rights of new states to decide for or against slavery without geographic restrictions. The bill passed and fueled the conflict between enslavers and abolitionists.**

# CHAPTER TWO

# 1821 TO 1840

**With the nation suddenly doubled in size,** anything seemed possible for one group of American citizens: wealthy white men. The nation's leadership believed that the United States had been chosen by God to grow and succeed beyond any previous measure. They were willing to sacrifice anyone and anything that might stand in the way of that divine destiny.

The future was bright for white men entitled to vote. But those living beneath that powerful class suffered many limitations. Women were not allowed to vote or own land or wealth. Even valuable gifts might belong to their fathers or husbands.

Black people were defined as three-fifths of a human being under the Constitution. They had fewer rights than white people in free states, and no rights at all in slave states. Poor white men and Indigenous People could count on some rights, but only if they agreed to live by laws that they weren't allowed to help make.

Freedom for all Americans had not yet been secured. But the desire for inclusion was expanding quickly and gaining strength—and not just in America. Revolution was spreading like wildfire, as France and South American colonies fought for independence from their royal rulers. All across the world, democracy was on the rise.

"America for the Americans" says this illustration

# The Monroe Doctrine: 1823

The United States wanted to be the strongest power in their part of the world, so they hoped to prevent other nations from establishing new colonies in North or South America. Great Britain shared the same goal, though for different reasons: If South Americans were free and independent from European powers, it would give Great Britain more opportunities for trade.

British diplomat George Canning suggested a new alliance between the United States and England. But just a decade earlier, Great Britain had been an enemy in the War of 1812. Could they be trusted as allies so soon? Secretary of State John Quincy Adams took the proposal to President James Monroe to decide.

Monroe was in favor of the alliance, as were former Presidents Thomas Jefferson and James Madison. But Adams feared the United

States would look weak—dependent on its old enemy. So he suggested a compromise that became known as the Monroe Doctrine.

On December 2, 1823, Monroe addressed Congress and made four announcements. First, the United States would not interfere in the affairs of foreign countries. Second, the United States would not interfere with existing foreign colonies in North or South America. Third, the United States would not allow the creation of *new* colonies in the Americas. And fourth, any attempt to control activities in the Americas would be seen as an invitation to declare war.

The European powers didn't take the doctrine seriously at first. Monroe could make demands, sure, but could he back them up? To fight the world, he would need a Navy, which the United States didn't yet have.

But even without fire power, the Monroe Doctrine set the stage for Manifest Destiny—the American conquest of land "from sea to shining sea," as the expression goes. Nothing would stand in the way of expansion, not even Indigenous Peoples that had lived on the continent for centuries. If God had blessed American expansion, then America's leaders believed they were entitled to do whatever it took to make it happen.

## SOUTH AMERICAN REVOLUTION

**When Napoléon Bonaparte conquered the Spanish monarchy and named his brother Joseph the new King of Spain, Spanish colonists in South America began to question their loyalties. Inspired by France and the United States, they launched revolutions of their own, forming independent nations across the Americas.**

The Battle of New Orleans

# The Election of Andrew Jackson: 1829

Before the 1820s, only white men who owned land and paid taxes could vote in American elections. But new states that joined the Union often allowed common men—white men without land or wealth—to vote as well.

Andrew Jackson was one of those common men. Raised poor in the Carolinas, he grew up rebellious but determined. At age thirteen, he was a messenger in the Revolutionary War. By age fourteen, he was an orphan, but he moved to Tennessee and became a successful lawyer and judge.

As a Major General of the Tennessee militia in 1802, Jackson was called "Old Hickory" due to his tough

Rachel Donelson Robards was a smart, divorced woman living with her mother after escaping an abusive husband. When Andrew Jackson met her, they fell in love and married—only to discover her first marriage had never legally ended. It was a scandal, but Jackson stood by his love and married her again in 1794 when her divorce was finalized.

style of leadership. It became his mission to drive Indigenous Peoples from their land to clear the way for white settlers.

Once promoted to the rank of Major General of the regular US Army, he faced a new challenge: leading men into the last battle of the War of 1812.

The War of 1812 was England's attempt to reverse the American Revolution. Jackson led a group of loyal soldiers, free Black men, Indigenous People, and pirates into battle against the British Redcoats—and shocked everyone by winning.

When Jackson ran for president in 1824, he ran as a man of the people and a war hero. Most people in the country voted for him—about 150,000 people. That was called the "popular" vote. Jackson also got

99 electoral votes, which were votes made by special representatives of each American state. About 100,000 people voted for John Quincy Adams, a wealthy northerner like presidents before him, and he won 84 electoral votes. But more than two people ran for president. Another man named Henry Clay won 37 electoral votes of his own. When he gave Adams his electoral votes, it was enough to beat Andrew Jackson. When he ran again in 1828, he won by a landslide.

For eight years, Jackson pushed back against the wealthy leaders of the past to help the average white American man. He fought against dishonest ways for the rich to get richer. He also set his sights on taking Indigenous land to create new white settlements.

In the end, Jackson's legacy was a patchwork of popular and unpopular choices.

## DEATH BY POISON BULLETS

**Andrew Jackson retired to his Hermitage Plantation in Tennessee after his presidency ended. His lifelong struggle with bad health took a turn for the worse and doctors made a startling diagnosis. Jackson had survived being shot twice, but the bullets were never removed. He died of lead poisoning on June 8, 1845, at the age of 78.**

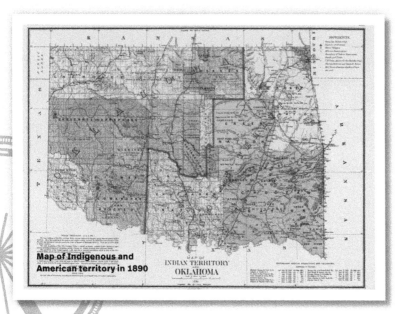

Map of Indigenous and American territory in 1890

MAP OF INDIAN TERRITORY OKLAHOMA

# Indian Removal Act: 1830

As the United States' population grew, so did the need for land. Influenced by the Monroe Doctrine, President Andrew Jackson saw it as his duty to secure that land.

Five tribes of Indigenous Peoples already lived on the land he wanted to use: the Cherokee, Choctaw, Chickasaw, Creek, and Seminole Nations. They joined together to resist the theft of their ancestral lands. The Wyandot, Kickapoo, Potawatomi, Shawnee, and Lenape tribes also stood to lose their homelands if Jackson got what he wanted.

Raised by a mother who saw Indigenous People as "savage," Jackson believed living in peace with the Indigenous Peoples would be impossible. So he proposed a solution called the Indian Removal Act of 1830.

Jackson suggested trading property in Oklahoma for land in seven southern states where these tribes already lived. He said the United States of America would pay to safely move the Indigenous People to their new homes, more than 500 miles west, in exchange for their cooperation. If some decided to stay on their land in the Southeast, they would be required to adopt the American lifestyle—including farming, paying taxes, and wearing white men's clothes.

Some Americans agreed the "Indian Problem" could be solved under the president's plan, but others were fiercely opposed. Debate raged among Congress, and the proposal barely passed. When it did, the treaties of the past suddenly didn't count anymore.

## MEET DAVY CROCKETT

For five months, the debate over the Indian Removal Act of 1830 raged on. One of its strongest opponents was Congressman Davy Crockett, who said he would never force his peaceful Chickasaw neighbors from their homes, not even for President Andrew Jackson. His opposition failed, but he stood strong for what he felt was right.

The Cherokee Nation wanted to fight the ruling and keep their homeland. They took their case to the United States Supreme Court in 1832. Supreme Court Chief Justice John Marshall and the other justices agreed that the existing treaties between the United States and the Indigenous Peoples had to be honored. The Cherokee could keep their land.

But Jackson refused to enforce this ruling, so tens of thousands of Indigenous People were forced to walk—some in chains, some at gunpoint—to land they had never seen, hundreds of miles away. As many as 25 percent of those people did not survive the dangerous journey and were hastily buried in shallow graves along the way.

## WHY FORCE INDIGENOUS PEOPLES TO MOVE?

Why were so many Americans willing to support Andrew Jackson's Indian Removal Act? Manifest Destiny. If God meant for the United States to expand, then any process to make this expansion happen could be justified. Removing Indigenous People freed up more than 25 million acres of farmland in Alabama, Arkansas, Florida, Georgia, North Carolina, Mississippi, and Tennessee, and the white settlers took it.

Cherokee Rose

# Trail of Tears: From 1830

According to their oral history—stories passed down for generations—the Cherokee Nation first encountered Europeans in 1540 when the Spaniard Hernando de Soto began his exploration of the southeastern region of what would become North America.

By 1827, the Cherokee had their own homeland, written language, newspaper, and constitution, separate from but approved by the United States of America. This all changed with President Andrew Jackson's Indian Removal Act of 1830.

The Cherokee watched as four other tribes were forced to abandon their homelands. Then a small group of Cherokee men betrayed their own people. Without

John Ross was the son of a Scottish father and a Cherokee mother. He helped run his grandfather's trading post in a suit and tie, but he also clung to his Cherokee roots. He was the Principal Chief of the Cherokee Nation from 1828 until his death in 1866.

permission, they signed the Treaty of New Echota, giving up what was left of the Cherokee land.

Principal Chief John Ross had been elected the Cherokee leader by more than 16,000 tribal citizens. He disputed the treaty, but Jackson ignored him. So did the president who came after him, Martin Van Buren.

In the fall of 1838, United States soldiers collected the Cherokee people at gunpoint and forced them into more than a dozen **concentration camps** with no more than the clothes they were wearing. White opportunists looted their homes and stole anything of value.

Days later, the Cherokee were made to walk the Trail of Tears—1,200 miles of rugged terrain from Georgia to Oklahoma. For nearly seven months, men, women, and children faced starvation, exhaustion, blinding rain, and snow up to their knees.

Witnesses along the path begged the soldiers to end the abusive march. Famous people like author Ralph Waldo Emerson called it a crime against humanity.

Government records say 4,000 Cherokee people died on the Trail of Tears. Cherokee historians believe the count was much higher. Those who survived worked hard to build a new nation once they arrived at their new home in March of 1839.

The Cherokee rebuilt their nation, but they never forgot their loved ones that died along the way—or the man who condemned them to death.

## CHEROKEE ROSES

According to Cherokee legend, when tribal elders prayed for strength on the Trail of Tears, the Heaven Dwellers promised a sign: Cherokee roses would grow along the path wherever grieving women wept. Their white petals would represent the Cherokee clans and gold centers represented the white man's greed. To this day, the flowers still bloom from Georgia to Oklahoma.

Peter Cooper's Tom Thumb railroad engine

# A Race Between Steam & Horse Power: 1830

As the American economy began to blossom, trade was everything. The ability to move goods from one place to another helped define who would succeed and who would fail.

Horse-drawn wagons were the most common mode of transportation. But roads could fail in bad weather. With a little rain, packed dirt could turn to mud. So experts explored new alternatives.

Rivers had always been used to ship products, but what if a boat could jump from one river to another? Cutting **canals** through existing land made that possible. But weather could freeze or flood the canals and shut them down, too.

Enterprising businessmen came up with a new idea: railroads. By embedding narrow, raised lengths of steel into the ground, horse-drawn cars could move along the tracks without fear of most weather conditions. And so the B&O Railroad was born.

The future of railroads seemed bright, but engineer Peter Cooper thought he could make it even brighter. Even sturdy draft horses could fail, and they had to be fed. Cooper wondered if railroad cars could be pulled by steam engines, instead.

He built *Tom Thumb*, a small locomotive, using a steam boiler that once powered a kitchen appliance and the metal piping from his musket barrels. On August 28, 1830, he staged a demonstration on a 13-mile stretch of track.

Observers marveled at the train's top speed: a whopping 18 miles per hour. It took *Tom Thumb* about an hour to cover 13 miles.

On the return trip, *Tom Thumb* met a horse-drawn car on the nearby track, and the race was on. Which would be faster, the steam engine or the horse?

The horse took the lead at first, because *Tom Thumb* had to build up steam. But once fired up, Cooper's train raced ahead. Passengers cheered, until a chain failed and *Tom Thumb* slowed to a stop.

By the time repairs were complete, the horse was victorious. But Cooper won in the end. B&O Railroad switched to steam power a year later and Cooper's improved technology increased railroad speeds to 30 miles per hour. Transport was becoming faster and easier than ever.

## REMATCH!

**According to the *Baltimore Sun* newspaper, B&O Railroad recreated the legendary race between *Tom Thumb* and the horse-drawn train in 1974 using replicas of the historic rivals. Yet again, the horse won—not once, but four times in a row.**

Battle of the Alamo in 1836

# The Texas Revolution: 1835 to 1836

Spain had been the first European nation to explore the **new world**, and the second to occupy Texas. But after the American Revolution, a wave of independence rolled across the continent, and Spain's colonial power began to fade.

When the United States bought the Louisiana Purchase from France in 1803, it included a small part of North Texas, but the rest belonged to New Spain. When Mexico won its independence from Spain, Texas became a Mexican state in 1821.

Mexico hired men called *empresarios* to convince Americans to move to Texas. So many Americans

## MEET ANTONIO LÓPEZ DE SANTA ANNA

The Mexican president who lost Texas to Sam Houston started his military career at age sixteen, siding with Spain to deny Mexico independence. When Mexico was free of Spanish rule, Santa Anna was elected president eleven different times. But he never put the people of Mexico first. Instead, he focused on what was best for himself.

bought Texas land, they were known as Texians. American soldier Sam Houston and former Congressman Davy Crockett were among the new Texian transplants.

Mexico then closed its borders and outlawed slavery. Texians were not happy, so US President Jackson offered to buy the state. Mexico refused.

Texians rebelled, and the region fell into chaos. Newly elected Mexican President Antonio López de Santa Anna became a dictator and slaughtered anyone who opposed him. He was willing to kill to keep Mexicans obedient. But he had a problem in Texas.

Texians rejected Santa Anna's bloodthirsty tactics and declared their independence in 1836. David Burnet was elected president of the Republic of Texas.

Sam Houston was named the Major General of the new Texas army.

Texas's fight for independence from Mexico ended with the Battle of San Jacinto. Sam Houston captured President Santa Anna and Burnet presented him with the Treaties of Velasco. It required Santa Anna to remove all Mexican forces from Texas and declare it an independent nation.

Santa Anna promised to defend the Republic of Texas's right to exist if Burnet set him free. But by the time Santa Anna returned to Mexico City, the Mexican capital, a new government had formed. The treaty was invalid because Santa Anna was no longer president.

President Burnet resigned when faced with the failed treaty. Sam Houston took his place and proclaimed the Republic of Texas would stand strong, with or without a treaty.

## REMEMBER THE ALAMO

As Texas fought for its independence, a group of 200 armed volunteers, including Davy Crockett, took cover in a **mission** now known as the Alamo. For thirteen days, they held off the Mexicans. They ultimately lost this battle, but the cry "Remember the Alamo" spurred Texas on to defeat the Mexicans.

# CHAPTER THREE

# 1841 TO 1860

**As the concept of freedom evolved in the United** States of America, more and more people began to rebel against its limits. The Declaration of Independence stated that "all men are created equal," but in practice, that wasn't true for everyone. Poor white men had to earn more wealth to enjoy true equality. Women and people of color had no pathway to equal standing at all.

Freedom had its price, and very few Americans could afford to buy it. But that was destined to change. People barred from the American dream were willing to fight to break down the barriers, even if they had to do it one small battle at a time.

Old ideas often die a slow and defiant death, but new ideas are required for a nation to grow. If America was going to live up to its potential, every citizen had to have at least a chance to succeed.

Thomas W. Dorr

# The Dorr Rebellion: 1841 to 1842

After the Revolutionary War, most American colonies abandoned the royal charters of King George in favor of new state constitutions. Rhode Island wasn't one of them. It kept following the rules written by the British rulers in 1663.

When the charter was written, white male citizens had been required to own land to be eligible to vote. But land was hard to come by in 1841 Rhode Island. Of the 26,000 adult white men living in the state, only 11,239—43 percent—were allowed to vote.

Thomas Wilson Dorr, a wealthy sympathizer, led a rebellion of men who wanted voting rights. He and his followers, called Dorrites, held their own "People's Constitutional Convention." Without any official authority, they wrote a new constitution and decreed that all white men over 21 could now vote, with or without land.

The Dorrites held an unauthorized election in April of 1842 to select a new governor of their own.

## MEET SAMUEL WARD KING

Samuel Ward King was born in Rhode Island in 1786. He studied at Brown University and graduated with a medical degree in 1807. He served as a military surgeon during the War of 1812 and later became the three-term Governor of Rhode Island. After he retired, Rhode Island did update their constitution, as the Dorrites demanded.

Unsurprisingly, Dorr himself won, even as Rhode Island's sitting governor Samuel Ward King won in the **legitimate** election. Now Rhode Island had two men claiming to be governor: one legal, and the other an illegal Dorrite.

When King refused to step down, the Dorrites planned an armed **insurrection**. Three hundred followers formed a **militia**. On May 17, they surrounded the state arsenal in the city of Providence and ordered Governor King to surrender. But their rebellion was defeated, and Dorr went into hiding in Connecticut while his followers were arrested.

But his efforts had an impact. After Governor King retired, Rhode Island agreed that extending voting rights made sense. They adopted a new constitution in November of 1842 that allowed all native-born American white men to vote without holding land. **Immigrant** white men still had to use the old rules until they were changed in 1888. Women, free Black men, and Indigenous People still couldn't vote.

Dorr returned to Rhode Island in 1843 after the new constitution was in place, only to be arrested and charged with treason. He spent a year in prison. Dorr died a folk hero in 1854 with a special grave marker added to his headstone. It read: "Governor Thomas Wilson Dorr, People's Constitution 1842."

## EXPANDING THE VOTE

Rhode Island saw the wisdom of suffrage—allowing more of its citizenship to vote—in 1842, but they were behind the curve. By the year 1840, approximately 90 percent of all white men were permitted to vote. Free Black men won the right in 1870, and white women could vote as of 1920, but it would be many more years before women of color could vote freely.

The Texas state flag over The Alamo

# Annexation of Texas: 1845

Almost as soon as Texas won its independence from Mexico in 1836, it asked to join the United States, a process known as **annexation**. If the United States agreed, Texas would receive military protection from Mexico, who wanted to retake the now independent territory. It would also expand the American border farther west.

But there were two big reasons for the United States to say no. First, Mexico had threatened war if Texas was annexed by the United States of America. And if Texas became a state, it would be another slave state in a nation divided by slavery.

## MEET SAM HOUSTON

Sam Houston was born in Virginia in 1793 and served under Andrew Jackson in the Battle of New Orleans. He moved to Texas in 1832 to start a new life in the Mexican frontier. Four years later, he was elected President of the Republic of Texas.

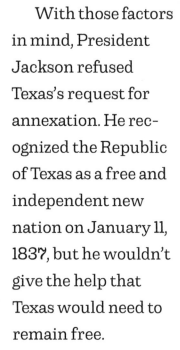

With those factors in mind, President Jackson refused Texas's request for annexation. He recognized the Republic of Texas as a free and independent new nation on January 11, 1837, but he wouldn't give the help that Texas would need to remain free.

Texas stood alone, facing military and financial uncertainty for nine more years. In that time, three American presidents took and left office without lending a hand. But still Texas clung to its freedom from Mexico.

On May 19, 1845, Mexico offered Texas a treaty. President John Tyler considered the offer, but the idea of annexing Texas had grown more and more popular in the United States. It was so popular by 1844 that Tyler was running for a second presidential term on the pledge of taking Texas in. So the president waited five months, then gave Mexico an answer: Thanks, but no thanks.

On December 16, Congress passed a joint resolution to annex the Republic of Texas for the United States of America. After Tyler lost to President James Polk, the news for Texas got even better: It was admitted into the Union as the 28th American state.

Anti-slavery activists were thunderously opposed to adding another slave-holding state to the Union, and Mexico still believed that parts of Texas belonged to them. Texas was officially an American state, but not everybody was willing to accept it.

## THE TEXAS CONSTITUTION

**The constitution of the Republic of Texas had some of the same elements as the US Constitution. But it had differences, too. In Texas, slavery was legal nationwide, and free Black people could only live there with special permission from the state's Congress.**

The Battle of Chapultepec in 1847

# The Mexican-American War: 1846 to 1848

With the help of President-Elect James Polk, President John Tyler finally convinced Congress to annex Texas, ignoring Mexico's threat of war.

But Polk had an even greater expansion in mind—one that would carry the United States territory all the way west to the Pacific Ocean. Leading Texas from annexation to statehood was his first step, but first there was a border challenge to overcome.

Texas claimed that its border extended to the Rio Grande River and included portions of modern-day New Mexico and Colorado. Mexico disagreed with that claim. They said Texas ended at the Nueces River, north of the Rio Grande.

President Polk took a bold stance in response to the disagreement. He sent the United States Army to Texas and they set up camp in the disputed territory between the Nueces and the Rio Grande rivers.

Next, he sent Congressman John Slidell to negotiate the purchase of the disputed land from Mexico. Mexico refused his offer of $30 million, and sparks began to fly between the US Army and Mexican loyalists in Texas. Polk used those skirmishes to convince Congress to declare war and violently take the land Mexico refused to surrender. And so the Mexican-American War began.

Many young officers experienced battle for the first time against Mexico, including Ulysses S. Grant and

## MEET ULYSSES S. GRANT

Ulysses S. Grant was born in Ohio in 1822, the son of a leather tanner. He studied at West Point, the United States military academy. As a young officer, he fought in the Mexican-American War, and later delivered victory to the Union Army in the Civil War. He was elected the 18th President of the United States in 1869.

Robert E. Lee, who would become famous generals in the future American Civil War. Though the US Army was outnumbered by Mexican forces, it was victorious when American General Winfield Scott stormed the capital of Mexico City and took control.

The Treaty of Guadalupe Hildago, signed on February 2, 1848, brought more than 525,000 square miles of territory under American control. That land would become Arizona, California, Colorado, Nevada, New Mexico, Oklahoma, Utah, and Wyoming. It cost just $15 million—half of what Slidell had offered Mexico.

Congressman David Wilmot tried to add a **provision** to the treaty that would ban slavery in the new territories. It was defeated, but the fighting it caused would extend all the way to the American Civil War.

## MEXICAN AMERICANS

When the United States of America claimed more than half of Mexico's territory, it also claimed part of its population. More than 80,000 citizens of the Republic of Mexico were suddenly in national limbo. They could move to land still under Mexican control, or they could become American citizens. But because they were not white, full American rights were not guaranteed.

Harriet Beecher Stowe

# Uncle Tom's Cabin: 1852

Born in Connecticut—a free state—in 1811, Harriet
Beecher Stowe was one of eleven children. Her parents, the Reverend Lyman Beecher and Roxana Foote
Beecher, taught their children to make the world
a better place. Writing would be Harriet's way of
inspiring change.

In 1832, the Beecher family moved to Ohio—also
a free state—where Harriet met and married her
husband, Calvin Stowe, and wrote professionally
part-time. A year later, she visited a nearby Kentucky
marketplace where she witnessed a **slave auction**.
A Black woman was sold before her eyes, torn away

The inspiration for the character of Uncle Tom was a man named Josiah Henson. Bought by a plantation owner named Isaac Riley in Rockville, Maryland, he escaped slavery and found freedom in Ontario, Canada. He fought to help enslaved people the rest of his life.

from her own child. It was an experience Beecher Stowe would never forget.

More than fifteen years later, the United States passed the Fugitive Slave Act to punish enslaved people who fled slave states for free states in the North. Where enslaved people who had escaped had previously found safety, they could now be hunted down for money and returned to their enslavers by force.

By then, the Stowes had moved to Maine, another free state. But a late-night knock on the door brought the issue to their doorstep. A Black man who had escaped slavery was seeking shelter. Offering sanctuary was against the law, but Beecher Stowe did not care. She let him stay.

After hearing about the abuses her guest had endured, Beecher Stowe prayed God would help her do something to fight the injustice.

When the publisher of *The National Era*, an anti-slavery newspaper, asked Beecher Stowe to write four stories about the cruelty of slavery in 1851, she remembered her guest's stories, then studied books written by formerly enslaved people as research. She didn't write four stories—she wrote forty.

Those stories became Harriet Beecher Stowe's famous novel, *Uncle Tom's Cabin; or, Life Among the Lowly*. Published on March 20, 1852, it sold 10,000 copies within a week. It went on to be one of the 19th century's bestselling books, second only to the Bible.

By creating the character of Uncle Tom—a loving, god-fearing man forced to endure the boundless cruelty of slavery—Beecher Stowe was able to make a lasting difference.

## HARRIET MEETS ABRAHAM LINCOLN

When Harriet met the 16th president on November 25, 1862, President Lincoln reportedly said, "So you are the little woman who wrote the book that started this great war." That may or may not be true, but there is little doubt—Harriet's work did help end slavery in America.

Dred Scott in 1857

# The Dred Scott Case: 1857

Dred Scott was born enslaved in Virginia around 1799. Peter Blow enslaved Scott until Blow's death in 1832. An army doctor named John Emerson bought Scott next. Eventually, Emerson and Scott moved to the free state of Wisconsin.

Wisconsin fell under the rules of the Missouri Compromise, which said that any enslaved person transported to Wisconsin was immediately entitled to their freedom. Scott was denied that benefit, but he did meet his wife, Harriet, in Wisconsin. Emerson allowed the couple to be legally married, and Harriet's enslaver gave the bride to Emerson so the couple could be together.

When Emerson moved to Louisiana and married Eliza Sanford, he took the Scotts with him. In 1843, Emerson died and his widow took possession of Dred and Harriet Scott, along with their two daughters. They tried to buy their freedom, but Sanford refused.

## MEET CHIEF JUSTICE ROGER TANEY

Roger Taney was born a rich, southern aristocrat and carried that background with him to the United States Supreme Court. Faithful to the enslaver's way of life, he made his belief that Black people were property into settled law in 1857. That ruling may have launched the Civil War.

The Scotts could not read and they had no money, but when they discovered that Dred should have been freed in Wisconsin, they decided to take Sanford to court. The Blow family who had once enslaved Scott offered to help.

The case was filed in April of 1846, but Dred Scott lost. He remained enslaved until he filed again in 1850 and won his freedom. But Sanford's brother **appealed** and the victory was overturned. The Scotts were once again enslaved.

In the end, the *Dred Scott v. Sanford* case went all the way to the United States Supreme Court. In March of 1857, Chief Justice Roger Taney ruled that all Black people in the United States, whether free or enslaved, were not citizens and could not make use of an American justice system reserved for citizens.

The Scotts' hopes were dashed—until Sanford remarried. Her second husband was fiercely opposed to slavery. So they sold the Scott family to Taylor Blow, the son of Dred Scott's first enslaver.

Young Blow granted the Scott family their freedom on May 26, 1857. Dred Scott died of tuberculosis a year later, but his family remained free for the rest of their lives thanks to his determination.

### WHAT'S IN A NAME?

Dred Scott landed in the history books for seeking his freedom as an enslaved person in America. But he might not have been named Dred at all. Some sources say his name was originally Sam Scott, and when his older brother Dred died, Sam took his name in tribute.

An armory at Harpers Ferry

# Harpers Ferry Raid: 1859

John Brown was born in Connecticut in 1800, and he grew up in Ohio. His religious family was very opposed to slavery. After Brown saw famous abolitionists Frederick Douglass and Sojourner Truth speak at the Free Church in Springfield, Massachusetts, he dedicated his life to ending slavery in the United States of America. Armed revolution was the path he planned to take.

One of Brown's first violent acts came in 1856 when the fate of slavery in Kansas was being decided. On May 21, pro-slavery forces raided the anti-slavery town of Lawrence. Brown and three of his sons arrived in Lawrence three days later, armed

with broadswords. Brown's sons took three pro-slavery advocates captive and cut them to ribbons. Brown put a bullet through the leader's head, just to be sure he was dead.

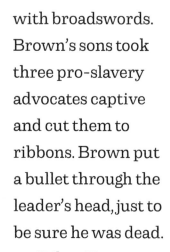

When Brown returned to Ohio, he raised money to launch his next offensive—arming enslaved people for an uprising. With the help of the "Secret Six," who were well-known abolitionists, Brown raised a small army of 22 men, including five Black men and three of his sons.

Brown's group rented a farmhouse near Harpers Ferry, a Virginia arsenal—a storehouse for weapons. They planned to steal the weapons inside to arm their slave rebellion. On October 16, 1859, Brown easily took control of the weapons, but he was quickly surrounded by a company of US Marines commanded by Robert E. Lee. With no way to escape, Brown's army decided to die for their cause instead of surrendering.

Ten of Brown's men, including two of his sons, were killed when Lee stormed the building. Brown was wounded, but survived to face his trial. Found guilty of treason and murder, he was sentenced to be hanged, but he showed no fear. As he stood on the gallows on December 2, 1859, Brown handed his guard a scrap of paper.

"I, John Brown, am now quite certain that the crimes of this guilty land will never be purged away but with blood," were his last words.

## ONE BLACK SURVIVOR

**Osborne Anderson was the only Black member of John Brown's army to survive the firefight at Harpers Ferry. He escaped to the safety of the North and wrote a book called *A Voice from Harpers Ferry* in 1861. The South had called him a criminal, but Anderson wanted to tell the other side of the story.**

# CHAPTER FOUR

# 1861
## TO
# 1880

**As the United States of America spread across** the North American continent, one big problem haunted its progress—slavery. Northern free states had lots of hard-working immigrants willing to farm food and create goods for a fair wage. The southern states had enslaved people.

Abolitionists fought for the end of slavery. Enslavers fought for their way of life. Neither seemed capable of compromise.

The numbers favored the free states in 1861 as Abraham Lincoln took office. Nineteen free states had representation in the House of Representatives and the Senate. Only 15 slave states stood against their majority votes.

Abraham Lincoln made his opinion crystal clear. "If slavery is not wrong," he wrote, "nothing is wrong." But his opinion didn't determine the law. The Constitution, the legislature, and the Supreme Court made the legal decisions.

Could Lincoln sway the other branches of government to see justice his way? And if he did, could he convince American citizens from all 34 states to respect and obey the laws his government created?

Slavery wasn't the only system of inequality plaguing America. Indigenous Peoples sought fair treaties, and women wanted the same rights as men. One thing was clear: America would either grow together or break apart.

Bombardment of Fort Sumter in 1861

# Southern Secession: 1860 to 1861

When Abraham Lincoln won the presidency in November of 1860, the southern slave-holding states refused to recognize his victory. Political leaders in the South met to discuss ways to protect the institution of slavery and to consider forming a new nation.

They drafted a constitutional amendment to prevent Congress from abolishing slavery where it was already legal. They also wanted to extend the Missouri Compromise to include new western states. And they wanted all new territories, North or South, to be considered pro-slavery.

When the states didn't ratify the amendment, South Carolina created a list of reasons showing that they had the right to secede (or withdraw) from the United States to form a new, pro-slavery nation. The longest paragraph covered the debate over escaped enslaved people and the right to recapture them.

Black enslaved people made up 60 percent of South Carolina's population. If they ran to freedom in the North and their enslavers could not recapture them, the state economy could fail. The Southerners argued that if the Union wouldn't let them retrieve runaway enslaved people, they would create a country of their own where slavery was legal everywhere.

By February of 1861, seven southern states—Alabama, Florida, Georgia, Louisiana, Mississippi, South Carolina, and Texas—had withdrawn from the union and formed a temporary government in Montgomery, Alabama. They named Jefferson Davis the president of this new Confederacy.

When the Southerners took over Fort Sumter, a defensive military base on the coast of Charleston, South Carolina, President Lincoln sent a supply ship to the **fortified** harbor with supplies. The Confederate rebels fired on the ship, and the Civil War officially began. Fort Sumter was destroyed in the fight.

Four more southern states—Arkansas, Virginia, Tennessee, and North Carolina—then joined the Confederate side. Four other slave states—Delaware, Kentucky, Maryland, and Missouri—sided with the North.

The Southern capital was moved to Richmond, Virginia, only 106 miles from the Northern capital in Washington, DC. Lincoln knew the only way to solve the country's problems was with a fight, but he hoped war wouldn't last long. But his hope didn't come true.

## FROM ONE VIRGINIA, TWO

As American states took sides, Virginia had a problem. Fifty counties within the western part of the state were loyal to the Union, not the South. When Virginia seceded, those counties seceded from Virginia to form West Virginia, a new Union state.

Battle of Gettysburg

# The Civil War: 1861 to 1865

As the Civil War started, it seemed the North would have a clear advantage. Soldiers from 23 free states fought for the Union Army. The Confederates only had soldiers from 11 slave states.

The north was also **industrialized**. They could make weapons, ammunition, railroad tracks, and engines with ease. And the Union Navy had gun-heavy new ships to launch by river and sea.

The South had agriculture, not industry. But they did have something the North did not have: desperation. If the South lost the war, they lost their entire way of life.

Thomas "Stonewall" Jackson was Confederate General Robert E. Lee's right-hand man. His men sometimes called him "Crazy Tom," due to his odd ways. He said eating pepper made his leg hurt, and he held one arm in the air to keep his blood flowing. He died after that arm was shot and cut off.

For more than two hundred years, plantation owners—who were only 25 percent of the South's white population—had grown rich off of Africans who worked from dawn to dusk planting and harvesting tobacco, sugar, rice, and cotton. The whole Southern economy depended on slave labor.

To defend that tradition, Confederate armies fought against the Union for four years in fierce, bloody battles, which left hundreds of thousands of bodies scattered across America. One side would claim victory in a battle, only to be defeated the next day or the next week. Territories fell into Union hands, only to be retaken by the South in the next fight.

Bloodbaths known as the Battle of Bull Run, the Battle of Antietam, the Battle of Fredericksburg, the

Battle of Seven Pines, the Battle of the Wilderness, the Battle of Gettysburg, the Battle of Vicksburg, and hundreds of others made victory and loss an endless string of deadly tugs-of-war.

Lifeless men littered every battlefield. Wounded arms and legs were amputated to prevent infection. Americans from both sides suffered incredible pain and horror to prove that their beliefs were right. But by the end of the war, they were all tired of fighting and death.

In the end, after 620,000 soldiers had died, it was Union General Ulysses S. Grant who accepted the surrender of Confederate General Robert E. Lee at the Appomattox Court House in Virginia. Enslaved people in the United States would finally know the taste of freedom.

## CIVIL WAR SURGEONS

**Hundreds of thousands of men were wounded in the Civil War, but they tried not to go to the hospitals for help. Surgeons at the time didn't really know how to heal their patients, so they experimented with amputations and other operations to find out.**

Black soldiers in the Civil War

# Emancipation Proclamation: 1863

As the Civil War raged on, President Abraham Lincoln felt pressure from the abolitionists. They wanted enslaved people to be freed immediately, but Lincoln couldn't deliver that.

Lincoln hated slavery. "There can be no moral right in connection with one man's making a slave of another," he said in 1854. But he wasn't the president of only the free states. He was the president of *all* the states. He had to consider both sides in his decisions.

Lincoln was also bound by the Constitution. He believed he could prevent slavery in new states, under the Constitution, but he could not ban slavery where it already existed. At first, the Civil War was about not expanding slavery into new states. But the abolitionists demanded more: making slavery illegal everywhere in America.

In the United States and in Europe, abolitionists were putting more and more pressure on their leaders to take stronger anti-slavery action. So in July of 1862, Lincoln met with his cabinet

One of the abolitionists advising Lincoln was Frederick Douglass. Born enslaved in 1818, he was taught to read by his enslaver's wife. He escaped slavery in 1838 and fought for **civil rights** the rest of his life. His words were so powerful, they helped redefine what it meant to be Black in the United States.

to discuss the **Emancipation** Proclamation. It would promise freedom to enslaved people living in the United States—including any Southern states if or when they rejoined the Union.

The proposal had cabinet support, but Lincoln's Secretary of State, William H. Seward, asked the president to wait for a Northern victory to make his announcement, then invite the Confederates to rejoin the Union.

On September 17, 1862, as the North was winning the Battle of Antietam, Lincoln delayed his advance on General Robert E. Lee in Maryland on the edge of victory. Five days later, Lincoln issued the Emancipation Proclamation. It wouldn't free all four million enslaved Americans, but it could inspire a revolution and show the abolitionists that Lincoln was working with them.

Southern states refused to rejoin the Union, but hundreds of enslaved people fled to the North seeking Lincoln's promised freedom. Hundreds of Northern citizens defied the Fugitive Slave Act and refused to return those people to their former enslavers.

Abolitionists saw the Emancipation Proclamation as a signal that Lincoln was no longer fighting only to reunite the country at any cost. He was now fighting to free enslaved Americans, too.

## FREE TO FIGHT

The Emancipation Proclamation was not Lincoln's only attempt to free the slaves. In July of 1862, Congress passed the Militia Act that gave Black men their freedom if they joined the Union army. More than 180,000 Black soldiers fought, and 16 won the Congressional Medal of Honor for bravery.

Celebration of the end of slavery in Washington, DC, in 1866

# Union Victory & Lincoln's Assassination: 1865

When the Union won the war, the Southern losses became crystal clear. Most big Confederate cities—the South's industrial centers—had been burned. Thousands of women had lost their husbands in the war.

At first, wealthy white Southerners had enslaved people to help them rebuild. But when news of the Thirteenth Amendment, which abolished slavery, made its way south, four million people were free to walk away.

The whole region had to be rebuilt without labor of enslaved people, and the South was lost and angry. Confederate **sympathizers** felt that Abraham Lincoln

Andrew Johnson grew up poor in Tennessee. As the Senator of Tennessee, he was the only Southern representative loyal to the Union during the Civil War. Six weeks after he was inaugurated Vice President, Johnson was sworn in to replace President Abraham Lincoln after he was assassinated.

should pay a price. One of these people was the actor and celebrity John Wilkes Booth.

When Lincoln went to a play at Ford's Theater on April 14, 1865, Booth saw his opportunity to get revenge for the South. As Lincoln sat in his presidential theater box above the stage, surrounded by his wife and friends, Booth loaded his pistol and waited.

When the audience cheered, Booth opened the door and took his shot.

The bullet pierced Lincoln's head below his left ear and he fell to the floor. The President's panicked companions blocked Booth's exit, so the assassin jumped down to the stage floor, breaking his ankle. As he shouted a message of revenge, Booth escaped.

The President's protectors carried him out of the theater. Once in the quiet of a nearby boarding house, the doctors found the bullet hole in Lincoln's head and realized he would not survive.

At 7:22 the next morning, the President of the United States took his last breath. Vice President Andrew Johnson became the new president four hours later.

Booth and his co-conspirator, David Herold, hid in swamps and barns as the Union Army searched the countryside for them. Confederate loyalists brought them food and newspapers. Booth expected the press to call him a hero. They called him a murderer instead.

Thanks to an anonymous tip, Union soldiers surrounded a barn where they were hiding and ordered the two men to surrender. Herold came out, but Booth refused. The soldiers set the barn on fire and shot at Booth inside. He died three hours later, whimpering, "Useless, useless."

## JUNETEENTH

The Thirteenth Amendment freed all enslaved people in the United States on January 31, 1865. But when Union soldiers got to the island of Galveston in Texas on June 19, no one knew it. That day, more than 250,000 people learned that they were freed, and a new holiday was born called Juneteenth. Today, 47 American states celebrate Juneteenth.

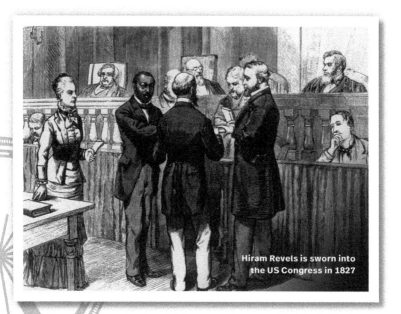
Hiram Revels is sworn into the US Congress in 1827

# Reconstruction: 1865 to 1877

The period after the Civil War is known as the Reconstruction Era. During this time, the United States worked to unite the North and South.

Passing the Thirteenth Amendment in January of 1865 was a big step toward these goals. This amendment said no man of any color could be forced to serve another man unless it was as punishment for a crime. Also in 1865, the Civil Rights Act promised citizenship to all people born in the United States, regardless of race or family heritage.

Four million Black Americans were suddenly free, but they now needed work, housing, and food. So Union

General William Tecumseh Sherman claimed 400,000 acres of land in South Carolina, Georgia, and Florida, broke it up into **homesteads**, and gave them to newly free Black men to make a fresh start.

When Lincoln was killed, Vice President Andrew Johnson was sworn in to take his place. But Lincoln and Johnson saw the future of America very differently. As the South began to rebuild, Johnson let former enslavers make new laws. He also revoked General Sherman's field order. Black homesteaders had to give their land back to the white men who had owned it before them.

Without land, newly freed people needed paying jobs. And landowners needed help. So **sharecropping** was born. Sharecroppers were given a piece of ground to farm and a house to live in. In exchange, they

## MEET SENATOR HIRAM REVELS

On February 25, 1870, Hiram Revels of Mississippi became the first Black American to win a seat in the United States Senate. Revel served on the Committee on Education and fought against **segregation** in schools. He worked to give other Black men a voice in politics, but also voted that Confederates should receive **amnesty** if they swore their loyalty to the Union.

had to give more than half the crops they farmed to the landowners.

To further control Black wage earners, Southern leaders established "Black Codes." These rules were the same as those once set for enslaved people, and Johnson supported them.

To push back, US legislators passed the Reconstruction Act in 1867 and the Fourteenth Amendment in 1868. The Reconstruction Act required Southern states to write new state constitutions, then allow their citizens to vote on them—including Black citizens. The Fourteenth Amendment gave all people born in the United States equal protections under the law, regardless of race. And in 1869 the Fifteenth Amendment was passed, making the right to vote a Constitutional guarantee.

People who had been enslaved finally had a real place in America, but the dream of true equality has been in progress ever since.

## FIRST BLACK CONGRESSMEN

**Six other Black men were elected to Congress in 1870. Alabama elected Benjamin Turner. Florida elected Josiah Walls. Georgia elected Jefferson Long, and South Carolina elected Robert DeLarge, Robert B. Elliot, and Joseph Rainey.**

Custer's Last Stand

# The Battle of Little Bighorn: 1876

As America expanded to the west, more Indigenous People were forced to abandon their ancestral homes. When they resisted, the United States Army Cavalry forces were sent to stop their rebellions.

When white men discovered gold on the Lakota reservation in South Dakota, they drove the Lakota out. Both they and the Cheyenne people were forced to flee to Montana.

Chief Sitting Bull of the Lakota and Chief Crazy Horse of the Oglala Lakota planned to hold council with other tribal nations. Here they would share ideas about how to preserve the old ways of their people and

## MEET SITTING BULL

 Sitting Bull was born in 1831 in what is now known as South Dakota. He was called Jumping Badger at birth. But after he hunted his first buffalo at 10 years old and joined his family on a raid at age 14, his father gave him a new name for his bravery: Tatanka Yotanka, translated as Sitting Bull.

plan for the white settlers that were sure to come.

In June 1876, 600 troops from the United States 7th Cavalry arrived in Montana, led by Lt. Colonel George Armstrong Custer, to stop the chiefs from holding their council.

Custer's men fought as the Army had taught them. First, they got off of their horses and handed the reins to a horse holder. Second, they lined up with their fellow soldiers, five yards apart. Third, they took a knee to steady their aim. Finally, they opened fire.

Twelve-hundred Indigenous defenders had different training. They fought on horseback, charging the American soldiers with speed and war cries. As their horses galloped, they fired guns and swung clubs or axes.

When both sides met on June 25, 1876, the attack was so fast and fierce, it caused a panic among the American soldiers. They ran for higher ground, but it was too late.

Within minutes, the Battle of Little Bighorn was over. All 259 men led by Custer were dead. Indigenous casualties were harder to count, but historians believe 31 men, 6 women, and 4 children died.

But the victory of the Indigenous People was short-lived. Five years later, the United States army completely removed the Lakota and Cheyenne from their land in Montana.

## CUSTER FAMILY LOSS

**Lt. Colonel George Armstrong Custer died in the Battle of Little Bighorn, but he was not the only member of his family to do so. Two of his brothers, his brother-in-law, and his nephew also died in the violent fight.**

# CHAPTER FIVE

# 1881
## TO
# 1900

**Newly freed Black Americans now had** protection under the law, but seeing those laws enforced was a different story. Many Southern whites and their Northern allies were not willing to extend Black Americans equality, regardless of the United States Constitution's new amendments.

Because states had a lot of power over their local laws and social norms, they created barriers to stop Black citizens from exercising their legal rights.

Most enslaved people had not been allowed to learn how to read or write while in captivity. So state and local governments set up literacy tests to prevent Black Americans from voting, renting houses, opening businesses, or landing jobs.

Black children were allowed to attend school, but not schools where white children were taught. Badly built schools with fewer resources were opened to serve Black children apart from the white students.

Transportation, restaurants, theaters, churches, and even water fountains kept Black and white Americans divided. With those divisions in place, it was difficult to learn that all races were equal and deserving of equal treatment and resources. That basic understanding was still decades away.

A Ku Klux Klan division in Watertown, NY, in around 1870

# Jim Crow Laws: 1880s

Jim Crow was a fictional character created by a racist entertainer to make fun of enslaved people in the 1830s. But the character's name took on new meaning when Southern states passed local laws that pushed back against the Constitution.

Those **racist** laws were soon called Jim Crow Laws. They were crippling and cruel to free Black citizens hoping to build new lives. If United States law said a Black man could claim a fair wage for hard work, the state law would make it legal to pay him less than a white man doing the same job.

If a Black man had the right to vote under federal law, local law would make it too hard or too expensive to do. Other local laws made Black men pay money to vote—but white men could vote for free. Because jobs were harder for Black Americans to find, most Black citizens didn't have that extra money, so they didn't get to vote. Their votes were **suppressed**.

If federal law said Black children could go to school, their Black-only schools were cold and poorly supplied, especially compared to schools for white children.

If Black people wanted to go out to dinner or see a show at the theater, they could not sit with the white customers. They were limited to bad seats or blocked from participating in other ways.

And Black people were punished more harshly than white people guilty of the same crimes. Even when they didn't break any laws, if they offended white people, citizen justice could be even more dangerous. White mobs beat Black people to teach them not to resist white dominance and control. Sometimes those racist crowds would resort to lynchings—hanging and killing Black people in public places in the dead of night. Fear of lynching kept many Black people from speaking out about injustices.

Others defied Jim Crow laws. They refused to give up, believing that freedom was worth any price racism might force them to pay. And they continue to fight. They are still fighting, even today.

## THE KU KLUX KLAN

**The Ku Klux Klan started as a social club for Confederate soldiers during the Civil War. But it slowly evolved into a terrorist organization determined to intimidate Black Americans in Southern communities. The KKK often threatened, beat, and even killed Black people, hoping to keep them from claiming their civil rights. They wore white robes and hoods to hide their identities from community members and the law.**

A cartoon of robber barons in 1885

# Robber Barons & Captains of Industry: 1880s

After the Civil War, the country's industrial potential exploded, and so did the opportunity to earn lots of money—especially if you were willing to cheat to do it. Men who used shady means to get rich came to be known as robber barons.

Cornelius Vanderbilt was one of the first robber barons. He started with a fleet of steamboats that brought people and goods from New York to New Jersey, and later expanded to ocean service. He drove his competitors out of business by charging far less money for his services.

One of the first American robber barons was fur trader John Jacob Astor, who cheated Indigenous People out of their animal pelts, then drove all other competition out of business, sometimes violently. He died the richest man in the United States in 1848. His great-grandson John Jacob Astor IV died on the luxury ocean liner *Titanic* 64 years later.

When he bought two railroads—the Hudson River Railroad and the New York Central Railroad—he gained great power. Two other robber barons, Jay Gould and James Fisk, cheated Vanderbilt out of buying the Erie Railroad. Even so, Vanderbilt died one of the richest men in America.

Jay Gould ran small businesses before he invested in the stock market on Wall Street and learned how to "corner" key markets through bribery and illegal trading. He and James Fisk tried to corner the gold market by lying to the President of the United States, Ulysses S. Grant. Their scheme caused the near collapse of the American economy on September 24, 1869—Black Friday—but they lost very little money of their own in the illegal trades.

Before James Fisk joined forces with Gould, he bought Confederate War bonds. The bonds were loans to help pay for the Southern war effort. If the South won the war, Fisk would get his money back, with **interest**.

Once he saw the South was losing, Fisk sold the war bonds to wealthy men in Europe who hadn't heard the news. Fisk walked away with a big profit. But when he argued with another man over an actress named Josie Mansfield, Fisk took a bullet and passed away. Cheating death wasn't as easy as cheating the living.

Men like Vanderbilt, Gould, and Fisk made no effort to share their wealth with the ordinary workers who kept their businesses running. That would change once the workers discovered they could make demands of their own.

## CAPTAINS OF INDUSTRY

**Some people consider rich men who cheat their way to success to be robber barons. But some call them "captains of industry." They see their ability to get huge amounts of money as inspirational. They did help turn the United States into an industrial giant, and that progress led the world to a bold new future.**

A bomb exploding at the Haymarket Square Riot in 1886

# Haymarket Riot: 1886

Big city factories were making rich men richer. But most workers were poor. People who had once farmed or made quality goods now worked ten-hour days, six days a week. There was no variety in factory jobs. Workers performed the same boring tasks, hour after hour after hour.

Worker safety didn't matter to most factory owners. Many paid politicians to stop safety rules from being enforced. Factory accidents killed as many as 35,000 workers each year. Many more were hurt so badly they could no longer work. Factory owners offered no pay to people hurt on the job.

The workers soon began to form **labor unions** like the Knights of Labor to convince the factory owners to pay more money and make the work safer. They also began to protest.

Two thousand people gathered in Chicago's Haymarket Square in Illinois to do just that on May 4, 1886. German immigrant August Spies climbed to the top of a hay wagon and talked about the "Eight Hour Movement," a plan for a shorter workday.

Albert Parsons spoke next. Parsons was a former Confederate soldier who fought for the rights of freed enslaved people after the war. He spoke calmly for about an hour—so calmly that the Chicago mayor, Carter Harrison, decided it was safe to leave the rally in peace.

Methodist preacher Samuel Fielden spoke last, after most of the people had gone home. For

## MEET LOUIS LINGG

Twenty-one-year-old Louis Lingg insisted he was not guilty of throwing a bomb at the Haymarket rally, but he confessed he was a **militant**. He was willing to fight for workers' rights, even violently, if it would guarantee safety and fair wages for the working poor.

20 minutes, he called the 200 remaining workers to action. His tone grew "wilder and more violent," according to one witness. Alarmed, 176 police officers moved in to clear the rest of the audience.

As the rally ended, someone threw a bomb into the crowd and it exploded. Armed with rifles, the police opened fire. Seven officers and one citizen were killed by bomb and bullets.

No one saw who threw the explosive, but police arrested eight labor movement men, including Albert Parsons and Samuel Fielden. All of them were found guilty and four were hanged. The Haymarket Riot went down in history.

## THE WORK CONTINUED

After her husband Albert was hanged in 1887, Lucy Parsons, a Black American radical activist, continued to work for the success of unions. She called for economic justice, women's rights, and rights for people of color until she died in a fire at her home in 1942.

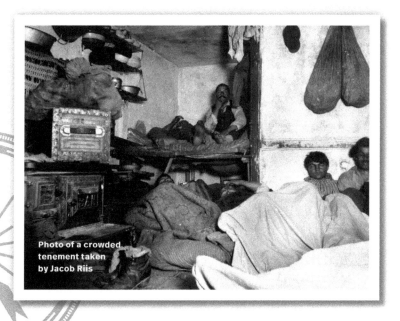

Photo of a crowded tenement taken by Jacob Riis

# How the Other Half Lives: 1890

Jacob Riis was only twenty-one years old when he left Denmark in 1870. He boarded the steamship *Iowa* in Glasgow, Scotland, with forty dollars, the clothes on his back, and a locket from the girl he left behind. He didn't know what he'd find when he got to America, but he was ready to find out.

Life in New York City was hard. For three years, Riis took any work he could find. Often homeless, he was forced to live in the poorest parts of the city with other struggling immigrants.

## MEET THEODORE ROOSEVELT

Theodore Roosevelt was one of six New York City police commissioners in 1895. He said, "No man is above the law, no man is below it; nor do we ask any man's permission when we require him to obey it. Obedience of the law is demanded as a right, not asked as a favor."

When he was hired as a police reporter in 1873, he met his destiny. Riis covered the Lower East Side where poor people were forced to sleep crowded on the floors of tiny rooms in **tenement** houses. One in ten babies born in those places didn't live to see their first birthdays.

The more Riis learned about the most dangerous parts of the city, and the more he saw the sick, the poor, and the vulnerable struggle, the more determined he was to help. That passion was clear in the stories he wrote.

Police commissioner Theodore Roosevelt admired Riis's journalism. He said Riis had "the great gift of making others see what he saw and feel what he felt." A close friendship grew between the reporter and Roosevelt, who would become the 26th president of the United States.

When Riis taught himself flash photography, he was able to share pictures along with his words. He published a book called *How the Other Half Lives* in 1890, filled with essays and images from the slums. It was an instant bestseller. Thanks to Jacob Riis, even the rich came to understand that life in the city's slums was unbearable.

Roosevelt soon called for housing reforms, saying, "The countless evils which lurk in the dark corners of our civic institutions, which stalk abroad in the slums, and have their permanent abode in the crowded tenement houses, have met in Mr. Riis the most formidable opponent ever encountered by them in New York City."

## OTHER RIIS BOOKS

*How the Other Half Lives* made Jacob Riis famous, but he continued to write books about the poor, including *The Children of the Poor* (1892), *Out of Mulberry Street* (1896), and *The Battle with the Slum* (1901). He also wrote an autobiography, *The Making of an American* (1901).

Forcing a Black man to leave the train in Philadelphia, 1856

# *Plessy v. Ferguson:* 1896

In 1890, the Louisiana state legislature passed the Separate Car Act. This law forced Black citizens to ride in separate train cars from those reserved for white citizens.

A group called the Citizens Committee decided to test the law through **civil disobedience**. One volunteer would break the law on purpose so lawyers could try its fairness in court.

Thirty-year-old shoemaker Homer Plessy volunteered because he was Black, by Louisiana law—one of his eight great-grandparents was black—but he looked white. He bought a first-class, whites-only ticket on the Louisiana Railroad on

June 7, 1892, and quietly took his seat.

When the train left New Orleans, conductor J.J. Dowling walked from seat to seat, asking each ticket holder if they were Black. When Plessy said he was, Dowling asked him to move to the Black passenger car. Plessy refused several times and was arrested for breaking the Separate Car Act. Plessy faced a fine of $25.00 and 20 days in prison.

## MEET JUSTICE JOHN HARLAN

When Supreme Court Justice Harlan disagreed with his fellow Justices, he became a beacon for future generations. "Our Constitution is color-blind," he wrote. "In this country, there is no superior, dominant ruling class of citizens." Harlan warned that the decision in *Plessy v. Ferguson* would sow the seeds of racial hatred.

The Citizens Committee paid Plessy's bail and he was released to await trial. Their plan had unfolded exactly as they had hoped it would.

A month later, Judge John Howard heard Committee lawyer Albion Winegar Tourgee's arguments. Tourgee said Plessy's Constitutional right to equal treatment under the law had been denied when he was asked to move. Judge Howard ruled that Louisiana law overruled the Constitution and found him guilty.

Four years later, Tourgee appealed Judge Howard's verdict before the United States Supreme Court. But seven out of eight Justices ruled that Louisiana's Separate Car Act could stand. The resources provided to Black and white people could be separate, the Supreme Court ruled, as long as they were equal.

They also ruled that Plessy was Black under the "one drop" rule, and could be reseated under Louisiana law. The guilty verdict would stand. Only one Supreme Court Justice, John Harlan, disagreed with the final decision.

Citizens Committee activists believed they had failed to advance Black equality that day. But they had given future activists a powerful new tool in civil disobedience. And as the United States' view of justice slowly caught up with the Constitution, many future cases would be won because of it.

## ONE DROP RULE

**Not all Americans were either white or Black. Many mixed-race people lived in the United States. Lawmakers said that any person with one drop of African blood was Black, no matter what they looked like.**

The battleship USS *Maine* in 1897

# The Spanish-American War: 1898

As the United States faced a new century, its people faced a new disagreement: Should America join other countries in the race to claim territory far from home, or should it stand up for freedom worldwide?

The question was tested when Spain sent 300,000 soldiers to their **colony** in Cuba, just 94 miles from the Florida coast. Cuba wanted independence, and Spain planned to knock the rebellion down.

Spanish General Valeriano Weyler—nicknamed "The Butcher"—put thousands of Cubans into concentration camps. He offered them "Subjugation or Death," and thousands soon died from starvation and disease.

## MEET ADMIRAL HYMAN G. RICKOVER

For more than 75 years, the United States blamed Spain for the destruction of the USS *Maine*. But in 1974, when Admiral Hyman G. Rickover called for a fresh review of the evidence, it cleared Spain of all responsibility. Coal stored too close to gunpowder in the *Maine*'s hull had caused the explosion. The Spanish-American War was launched based on a mistake.

American newspapers published by William Randolph Hearst and Joseph Pulitzer ran dramatic headlines and graphic cartoons of the Cubans' suffering and encouraged Americans to consider war with Spain.

President William McKinley, who had fought in the Civil War, hoped to find a **diplomatic** solution. But American lives were in danger, too. Wealthy US investors had spent $50 million to grow sugar in the rich tropical farmland. They were in Cuba to manage the plantations.

In January of 1898, McKinley sent the USS *Maine*—America's first steel battleship—to the harbor of Havana, Cuba, just in case Americans had to leave. But he asked the captain to keep the visit friendly, still trying to prevent a war.

For more than two weeks, the *Maine* was peacefully docked. But at 9:40 p.m. on February 15, 1898, disaster struck. As 350 crewmen slept, an explosion sank the battleship, and 266 Americans died.

Newspaper headlines like "The Warship *Maine* was Split in Two by an Enemy's Infernal Machine" made Americans eager to fight back. McKinley was forced to take action. He demanded that Spain leave Cuba. When Spain refused, Congress declared war.

In just three months, three weeks, and two days, the United States defeated Spain. The Treaty of Paris was signed on December 10, 1898. Spain gave Cuba its freedom and released Guam and Puerto Rico to the United States. For a $20 million fee, the United States gained control of the Philippines, too.

The United States of America had proven it was a genuine world power. That proof discouraged any new North American invasions by outside forces.

## T.R. AND THE ROUGH RIDERS

**When the Spanish-American War broke out, Theodore Roosevelt resigned as Assistant Secretary of the Navy to fight. His team of rowdy cowboys, college athletes, and Indigenous Peoples was officially known as the First US Volunteer Cavalry, but Roosevelt called them his Rough Riders and led them to battle from atop his horse, named Texas.**

# LOOKING AHEAD

Some important changes don't come quickly. And many changes that took root in the 19th century were as important as they could get.

Enslaved Africans forced to leave their homes for a land across the sea grew tired of being enslaved. Working for cruel enslavers nearly broke them. And still, they dreamt of change—of freedom. They risked their lives to make that change happen.

Bold American explorers traveled far and wide, making maps of land they'd never seen before. They wondered, could the United States of America expand beyond its original borders?

Indigenous Peoples who already called those places home were promised friendship that changed to violent betrayal. They worried that their way of life would disappear forever.

New laws brought the hope of change to some Americans. But others saw those changes as impossible to accept. When differences could not be settled with words or reason, a winner was decided by war.

Bloody battles changed almost every American who fought in them. They raged on and on and claimed thousands of lives. Who would come home when war ended? Who would be forever lost?

Even after victory was won, some people resisted change. It came, but slowly . . . very slowly. Some 19th century struggles continue even today. Working so hard, for so long, can be discouraging. But history marches on.

If the change you seek is taking too long, remember, you are not alone. Study the past and you'll find a team of allies whispering words of encouragement. Let their determination give you hope, too.

# GLOSSARY

**abolitionist:** A person who works to end something

**alliance:** Union between two or more parties

**amendment:** Addition or change

**amnesty:** Official forgiveness

**annexation:** The process of adding or joining one piece of land with another

**appeal:** To ask to reconsider a legal decision

**bilingual:** Able to speak two different languages

**botany:** The study of plant life

**canal:** An artificial waterway

**chief:** Leader, often of a tribe or nation of Indigenous Peoples

**civil disobedience:** Peacefully refusing to follow a law as a form of protest

**civil rights:** Rights promised by the government or the law

**colony:** Land that is owned by a country, usually a country that is far away.

**concentration camp:** A place where government imprisons dissenters or minorities

**dictator:** One person controlling many others

**diplomatic:** Use of words to solve a problem

**emancipation:** Being freed from the control of another person or entity

**homestead:** An area of land provided to a family

**human rights:** Freedoms, opportunities, and resources that belong to every person

**immigrant:** A person born in one country who moves to another country and settles there

**industrialized:** Mechanically developed

**insurrection:** An uprising against the government

**interest:** Extra money paid for the temporary use of someone else's money

**labor union:** A group of workers who organize in order to protect their rights

**legitimate:** Allowed by the law

**militant:** Someone who takes action with aggression

**militia:** An unofficial armed group of people

**mission:** Church outposts used to spread Christianity

**new world:** The Western Hemisphere, primarily the Americas

**racist:** A person or thought that believes one race is better than another

**rebellion:** The act of going against an authority

**segregation:** The separation of groups of people

**sharecropping:** The system of tenants farming land and giving a percentage of crops to the landowner as rent

**slave auction:** A market at which enslaved people were sold to whichever buyer offered the most money

**suppressed:** Forcibly stopped, prevented, or silenced

**sympathizers:** People who understand how you feel

**tenement:** An apartment building

**terrorist:** A person who uses violence to create an atmosphere of fear and to get their way

**treaty:** Written agreement between countries

# RESOURCES

## Books

Bruchac, Joseph. *The Trail of Tears*. New York: Random House, 1999.

DK Editorial Team. *DK Eyewitness Books: Civil War*. New York: DK /Penguin Random House, 2015.

Herman, Gail. *Who Was Davy Crockett?* New York: Penguin Workshop, 2013.

MacDonald, Fiona. *Women in 19th Century America*. Chicago: Peter Bedrick Publisher, 2001.

Rappaport, Doreen. *No More!: Stories and Songs of Slave Resistance*. Somerville, MA: Candlewick Press, 2005.

## Museums

Abraham Lincoln Presidential Library and Museum (Springfield, Illinois): ALPLM.org

American Civil War Museum (Richmond, Virginia): ACWM.org

National Museum of African American History and Culture (Washington, DC): NMAAHC.si.edu

National Museum of American History/Smithsonian Institution (Washington, DC): AmericanHistory.si.edu

Thomas Jefferson's Monticello (Charlottesville, Virginia): Monticello.org

# SELECTED REFERENCES

Africans in America. "Dred Scott's fight for freedom." PBS. 2020. Retrieved October 14, 2020. PBS.org/wgbh/aia/part4/4p2932.html.

Alfred, Randy. "Sept. 18, 1830: Horse Beats Iron Horse, for the Time Being." *Wired*. September 7, 2008. Retrieved October 14, 2020. wired.com/2008/09/sept-18-1830-horse-beats-iron-horse-for-the-time-being.

American Experience. "Plessy v. Ferguson." PBS. Retrieved October 14, 2020. PBS.org/wgbh/americanexperience/features/neworleans-plessy-v-ferguson.

American Experience. "The Mexican American War." PBS. Retrieved October 14, 2020. PBS.org/wgbh/americanexperience/features/grant-mexican-american-war.

Blount, Roy, Jr. "The Civil War: Making Sense of Robert E. Lee." *Smithsonian Magazine*. July 2003. Retrieved October 14, 2020. SmithsonianMag.com/history/making-sense-of-robert-e-lee-85017563.

Bragg, Meredith. "The Raid on Harpers Ferry." *Smithsonian Magazine*. 2020. Retrieved October 14, 2020. SmithsonianMag.com/videos/category/history/the-raid-on-harpers-ferry.

Brockell, Gillian. "Gabriel's revolt: In 1800, he was savvy, armed and determined to end slavery in Virginia's capital." *The Washington Post*. August 23, 2019. Retrieved October 15, 2020. WashingtonPost.com/history/2019/08/23/gabriels-revolt-he-was-savvy-armed-determined-end-slavery-virginias-capital.

Cherokee Nation. "History." 2020. Retrieved October 14, 2020. Cherokee.org/About-The-Nation/History.

Gist, Lestey. "Black Abolitionists: Osborne Anderson The Only African American to Survive." February 23, 2020. Retrieved October 14, 2020. BlackThen.com/black-abolitionists-osborne-anderson-african-american-survive.

Harriss, Joseph A. "How the Louisiana Purchase Changed the World." *Smithsonian Magazine.* 2003. Retrieved October 15, 2020. SmithsonianMag.com/history/how-the-louisiana-purchase-changed-the-world-79715124.

Jim Crow Museum of Racist Memorabilia. "The Origins of Jim Crow." Ferris State University. Retrieved October 3, 2020. Ferris.edu/htmls/news/jimcrow/origins.htm.

Micalizio, Caryl-Sue. "May 28, 1830 CE: Indian Removal Act." *National Geographic.* April 6, 2020. Retrieved October 14, 2020. NationalGeographic.org/thisday/may28/indian-removal-act.

New England Historical Society. "The Dorr Rebellion: When RI Had 2 Governors." Retrieved October 14, 2020. NewEnglandHistoricalSociety.com/dorr-rebellion-ri-2-governors.

Northern Cherokee Nation. "The Legend of the Cherokee Rose." 2020. Retrieved October 14, 2020. NorthernCherokeeNation.com/the-legend-of-the-cherokee-rose.html.

PBS. "Lewis & Clark: The First American Expedition." May 1, 2017. Retrieved October 14, 2020. PBS.org/video/first-american-expedition-onrro9.

Richardson, Sarah. "The History of the Real Jim Crow." HistoryNet. April 2018. Retrieved October 3, 2020. HistoryNet.com/as-american-as-jim-crow.htm.

# ABOUT THE AUTHOR

 **Kelly Milner Halls** lives in Spokane, Washington, with two daughters and too many pets. She has written nonfiction for young readers for more than 25 years. Each book she writes teaches her more about the world. She hopes each book you read will do the same for you.

9 781648 768156